God?

ANDY ACHESON

who is God?

AND WHY IT MATTERS

10 Publishing
a division of 10 of those.com

British Library Cataloguing in Publication Data

A record for this book is available from the British Library

ISBN: 9781837280353

Designed by Jude May
Cover image © Normform | iStock

Printed in Denmark

10Publishing, a division of 10ofthose.com
Unit C, Tomlinson Road, Leyland, PR25 2DY, England
info@10ofthose.com
www.10ofthose.com
1 3 5 7 10 8 6 4 2

For my precious daughters, Lydia, Noá and Phoebe.

I want nothing more than for you to know the God this book is about.

Contents

Introduction

Why Should I Bother Reading This?

The last few years have been a bit much, haven't they?

Life in the world today so often feels chaotic, confusing, disorientating, and even a little disturbing. One disaster seems to roll into the next, and with every refresh of the page another news story appears, sometimes more shocking than the last. Whether it's Putin, or a pandemic, or a personal tragedy, the world seems to be spiralling and spinning out of control in all sorts of ways.

Take for example the environment. Evidence of climate change just keeps on growing, but no one seems to care enough to help. Who's even in charge of this planet? And it's not just the environment that seems to be out of control …

It seems impossible to scroll down our feeds without seeing war and conflict in all sorts of places around our world. One day children play happily and the very next day goalposts are driven over by 40-tonne tanks. People hide in basements and bunkers as bombs and bullets rain down.

For lots of us suffering is far closer to home. Our cities and towns are bursting with blades; teenagers seemed to be attacked all the time. For some, the bleeps and beeps of hospital wards form the soundtrack to our sadness. Cancer. Disease. Heart problems. Brain tumours. Anxiety. Depression. The list goes on.

Then there's the internet which seems to be a Wild West, where no one really rules and we all have to watch our own backs. Artificial intelligence can put words in anyone's mouth, footage is doctored and it's impossible to know what is true and who we can trust. Chatbots have all the answers but how do I ever know when I'm talking to a person or a machine? Technology never seems to be satisfied; it's exhausting.

How can we *not* feel worried and anxious in a world like this one?

* * *

A few months back my family and I were on a flight and I was sitting between my 4-year-old and 6-year-old daughters. The weather wasn't great and, as it turned out, our plane was the last one allowed to leave before the rest of the flights were grounded due to very high winds. We hit serious turbulence. You know the sort where the flight attendants stop trying to sell you stuff and sit down, strap their seatbelts on tight and make uneasy eye contact with each other? That sort of turbulence.

My little girls were worried, gripping my hands as our plane shuddered through the sky. But then the pilot spoke to us. He assured us all was fine; it was a bit windy but nothing to worry about – he'd been in much worse weather than this before and never had an issue. Instantly I felt the grip on my hands loosen. My four-year-old smiled at me, she said, "It's okay daddy, the pilot said we don't need to worry!" And that was more than enough for the girls. They stopped cutting off the blood supply to my fingers and started asking me for sweets and whether we could get McDonald's on the drive home. It was a total game changer.

When everything around us feels noisy and messy and busy and scary – when the world feels totally out of control – we are prone to panic. How could we not? But what we need is someone who is bigger than us. Someone who knows better than us. Someone who can give us peace in the chaos. Someone who has been around longer than us, who has seen it all before, and who can keep us safe.

If we are going to be honest about the world around us – rather than block it out – the only thing that can stop us freaking out is to get to know God better. He made this world, and he rules this world, and as we get to know him more, we'll trust him more.

This book is all about the God who makes sense out of stress, and brings clarity to chaos. We're going to think about who God is and what he is like. We're going to see how really getting to know God helps us to make sense of what he is doing and has done in our world.

We'll see that he does what he does because he is who he is.

If you wouldn't call yourself a Christian, why not allow this book to tell you more about the God you're trying to make up your mind about? What you believe about God is the most important decision you'll ever make, so you need to know who it is you're considering rejecting or following!

For those of us who already believe in him, this book will hopefully help you get to know him better. And as we do that, panic will be replaced by prayer. Fear by faith. Confusion by confidence.

Let's get to it!

Chapter 1

God is Love

There is so much suffering. And not just in an "out there, far away" sort of way. The brokenness is all around us, isn't it?

Marriages collapse; grandparents die; depression is everywhere.

Is God there? Is God fair? Does God care?

How am I supposed to hold the idea of a good God *and* suffering in my head at the same time?

* * *

We hear people say: "There can't be a God because of all I've gone through", or "If God exists I don't want to know him because of what happened to me." I get it. It's tempting to think that way. It's natural to look at experience, draw conclusions based on what we see, and adjust our view of God in light of that.

Suffering is a massive problem. But if you start with the problem and try and work everything out from that, you can end up with a wrong conclusion.

For example, when my wife Katie was little she came to the conclusion that paving stones bled! After all, when she fell on the grass nothing much happened, but when she fell on the path there was blood on her knee. Totally the wrong conclusion. If you start in the wrong place, you'll very easily end at the wrong place too. Like buttoning a shirt, if you start out of kilter, you'll get every button wrong.

Instead of beginning with the problem, this book will start with God and try to understand the world in the light of who he is. And the first thing we need to know about him is that "God is love" (1 John 4:16).

* * *

Our society thinks it's got love sorted.

We love "love". All you need is love!

Love is in charge. Love is king. In fact, our world would say: "Love is God." There's nothing higher or better or more important. But what does "love" actually mean?

You hear about love all the time. We can't stop saying we love things: People, pets, movies, songs, stories, books, binge-watching, McDonald's, memes. We heart emoji so many posts online each day that we can't even count them. But talked about like this, love has become so diluted it barely means anything anymore.

Have you ever been camping? Imagine you pack your things up – you have your rucksack filled with food, water, matches, maybe even some soap. Tucked under one arm is a sleeping bag and under your other is a tent.

And this isn't any old tent, it's a tent you remember playing in as a kid. It's sheltered you from the sun and has withstood years of summer holidays. Why wouldn't you take it on your camping trip?

The thing is, though, it's a beach tent. Perfect for days at the seaside but not for overnight stays up the side of a mountain in winter. When the storm breaks and the heavy wind blows you quickly realise that even though the beach tent worked perfectly well on sunny days, when it comes to a tough moment it's not very good after all.

That's what the idea that we can love everything is like. It doesn't hold when you push it. It falls apart, because on the hard days there's nothing solid or satisfying about emoji love. Ever-present, everything love seems to disappear pretty quickly when things get tough. We need a stronger kind of love than the one we feel for some new fluffy socks or a photo on Snapchat.

While the world says: "Love is God", but never really explains what that means, the Bible puts it the other way round.

* * *

Two thousand years ago, the disciple John wrote his three-word definition of love – catchy, simple and wonderfully rich:

> "… **God is love**. This is how God showed his love among us: He sent his one and only Son into the world that we might live through him. This is love: not that we loved God, but that he loved us and sent his Son as an atoning sacrifice for our sins." (1 John 4:8–10, emphasis mine)

See where love comes from? God! It begins with God.

Every little bit of love we've ever known or experienced comes from him. Love is his thing. Love is who he is. God is only, ever and always loving because he is always love.

You can see God's loving nature and his loving actions in a huge variety of ways but here in 1 John we see the ultimate way God revealed himself to us and showed us his love: he sent his one and only Son Jesus into the world.

God's love isn't distant or confusing or uncertain. He showed his love for us in the most incredibly "reach out and touch it" kind of way, when he sent his Son Jesus into our world.

He met people. He taught people. He prayed for people.

He healed people. He fed people. He ate with people. He laughed with people. He wept with people. He did life up close and personal with people.

His love was costly. After all God didn't send Jesus into a different world, or a better world, or an easier world. The world was just as bad back then as it is now. When Jesus was born a dictator just as evil as any we have today, Herod, commanded that all baby boys under two should be killed. Jesus quickly became a refugee (at least that's what we'd call it today), fleeing to Egypt in his parents' arms, just in order to survive. Jesus experienced rejection and pain. He was mocked, abused, belittled, rejected and ignored. He knew death all too well.

All the pain and sadness this world contains was seen, experienced and felt by God himself in the person of his Son Jesus Christ. When it comes to suffering *God gets it*. All of it. He knows how you feel when you cry those hot tears of pain; he's cried them himself.

The God-who-is-love came to this world, wrapped in flesh, in his Son, Jesus.

* * *

The Apostle John also tells us Jesus came to the world to save us. God "loved us and sent his Son as an atoning sacrifice for our sins" (1 John 4:10). That's the central message of the Christian faith. That's the gospel, which literally means good news.

But in order to reach that good news, first we have to stomach some hard home truths. We have to accept the reality that each and every one of us left to ourselves would never choose to love God. Actually left to ourselves we would always choose to love ourselves and we end up lost and broken.

It goes back to Adam and Eve in the Garden of Eden. We read in Genesis 3 about how these first humans rejected God, in what Christians now call "the Fall". The truth is that all of us, if we'd been in Eden, would have done as they did. We all have this thing inside us that pushes God away and wants to rule over our own hearts and lives. The Bible calls that sin. Sin is all about not loving God and his good ways:

- Sin is primarily to do with how we act towards God but it has huge impact on the way we treat other people around us.

- Sin is both what we choose to do (that we shouldn't), and what we choose not to do (when we know we should).
- Sin leaves us cut off from God, not able to enjoy relationship with him, and without hope of spending eternity with him either.
- Sin is shown in our actions, but it actually reveals our nature.

Why is it such a big deal? Well because God is light, he is the opposite of sin. He is love. He is all that is good and right. He is perfect, and can no more be around our sinfulness than light can be around darkness. God and sin can't go together.

Sin destroys our relationship with God and leaves us spiritually dead if we don't trust in Jesus. It's that big a deal.

All of that is why it's such incredible news that God sent his Son Jesus to be the sacrifice for our sins. Jesus died in our place, for our sins, to pay the price for us so that we can know and enjoy God's love.

> "God demonstrates his own love for us in this: while we were still sinners, Christ died for us." (Romans 5:8)

When we become Christians, we are no longer defined by our sin, instead we are defined by his love. We are no longer God's enemies, instead we become his loved, chosen children. I don't know where you are as you read this, but this is jump up and down, scream and shout, "we just won the cup final" level good news.

It might be worth grabbing a Bible and opening up 1 John 4 and reading verses 7 to 21 because there is so much more wonderful stuff in there. (If you don't have a Bible nearby just Google 1 John 4 and you'll get it.) The passage is incredible.

Everything there is to know about God, everything there is to say about God, everything God has ever done comes from the overflow of his relentless, endless, unconquerable, inexhaustible bottomless love.

* * *

I've got three young daughters, and I never knew I could feel anything half as powerful as the love I feel for them. When they're happy I can't stop smiling. When they're sad I become utterly pathetic. They drive me crazy and yet I adore them. When something isn't right in their lives, I sit up at night worried about them. When there's something they want I daydream about how I can afford to get it for them. I just love them so much. And not because they've done anything impressive or deserving, it's actually normally in spite of that – sometimes young children can be really hard work.

But when a parent loves their child, then everything they do for them comes from a place of love, even if it doesn't seem that way to their son or daughter.

Sometimes parents show their children love with a big cuddle, and kind words. At other times they show love by being really strict ("You must wear your seatbelt"). Other times they show love by giving their kids freedom to make mistakes, even if they can see what's coming!

God is the ultimate Father. Unlike earthly dads, he never messes up and always acts out of love.

He always acts in love, because that's who he is. But just like little children don't always understand their dad's loving actions, sometimes we can find God's actions surprising and confusing. Sometimes it can be really painful when he knows what's best for us but we can't see it. Sometimes when he gives us freedom to make bad decisions and those choices impact on others, it's hard to understand what he's doing. And when we see that on a global scale it can be even harder to stomach.

When I've tried to explain to my kids why I've decided things need to be a certain way, occasionally they still don't get it. They get cross that I don't let them do things they want to do, and disappointed that I'm not willing to do certain things for them. I have felt all of those things about God myself. I still do sometimes.

There will be times when we have to accept that we don't get it, that God is allowing people to do things when we really don't think he should. Sometimes God isn't doing things the way we would like and that's okay. If God is God then we have to let God be God, even when it stings. But it's so important to remember that our up-and-down emotions don't change who God is – we don't have that kind of power.

God is love. He always has been. He always will be. It's who he is.

So what?

You might be thinking: that's all well and good, but how does it help me? We're still in a world of suffering.

If God is love then why does life hurt so much? Why does the idea that "God is love" matter when we feel heartbroken as we face yet another crushing disappointment or loss?

Well, firstly, while it's always awful when tragedy comes, we should never really be surprised that this world is full of pain, because we know this world is full of sin. When people like me and you choose to turn our backs on God, rejecting his love and his good ways and instead follow our own ways, the world gets darker. But the sin in the world should never be evidence against God's love. Sin actually leads to the ultimate evidence for God's love! In God's response to sin, we see his love made flesh in Jesus entering our broken world. He could have turned his back on us but he didn't. That's real love. Doing love. Refusing-to-give-up-on-us love. Giving-everything-for-us love.

And what's even more incredible: Jesus hasn't gone back to heaven for good. One day he will return to get rid of sin forever. There will be a day where there is no more suffering, pain, tears or hardship. Crying, dying and lying will be distant memories on the shores of eternity.

But what about today? What comfort is there right now? Well we can have hope that no matter how hard or sad things feel like they are getting, God loves us, and his love isn't going to ever go away no matter how awful we feel. We can be confident he'll never walk out on us. We can be sure he'll carry us through. No matter what happens to us. No matter how much our lives change. He never will.

So no matter how tragic our circumstances are, no matter how deep our loss is, no matter how crippling the pain in our bodies, we still have hope and joy because God is right there with us and he's good and kind and full of love. No matter where we are standing, whether it's on a mountaintop or at a graveside, God's love is dependable. And if we're ever tempted to doubt his love, if we're ever tempted to think that human pain, tragedy, suffering, loss and death can't go hand in hand with God then we need to look no further than the cross on which Jesus died. As Jesus experienced the worst pain, loss and suffering imaginable, God was present and working in and through every single bit of it.

On the day Jesus hung on the cross, God's love was written in his hands, feet and sides for the whole world to see. So on the days where we feel our deepest sadness and pain we can be sure that God is love all the same.

God is love, you can know that and you can rely on that. Always. Forever.

Chapter 2

God is Three-in-One

You see it all the time in sporting events: fans folding their hands, praying for victory. When in a crisis most of us will silently plead for help. The moment tragedy strikes anywhere in our world, it takes mere seconds for the latest hashtag to be unfurled: #PRAY. There's something written into our DNA that causes us to pray – even for people who say they don't believe in God!

But here's the problem. We pray … and what we ask for doesn't happen. Sometimes we keep on praying … and it keeps on not happening.

Why don't my prayers work? Why should I trust a God who doesn't seem to listen or act in my life? It's hard to feel interested in him when he doesn't seem to be interested in me.

And what's all this got to do with the Trinity?

* * *

There are some things in life I just don't understand. Take planes staying up in the air for example. It's got something to do with lift and thrust overcoming drag and gravity, and I'm pretty sure the pilot has to pull a lever or two ... But I don't really have a clue how they do it. Yet every time I fly, I trust my whole life to my belief that planes do stay up. I just take it as a given. I nod and smile, sit back, eat some fruit pastilles, and assume that cleverer people have worked it all out.

When it comes to God being Trinity – Father, Son and Holy Spirit, yet one God – it's easy to have a nod-and-smile approach too, isn't it? We can accept the church believes in the Trinity, know that it's really important, and yet just assume that cleverer people have got it worked out and we don't need to think about it.

But while it doesn't really matter if I don't bother to understand aeronautical engineering, it matters enormously if I don't take time to consider who God is. After all, the very reason I exist is to know God. That's why he made me. And the only way to know life to the full is to spend my life enjoying him. Plus without knowing who he really is, I'll never know who I really am, because he made me in his image.

Often we can assume knowing God as Three-in-One is like the absolute top level of where we might end up one day if we get really strong in our faith. Trinity is like Master's degree level faith and we're only supposed to be at GCSE right now. But that's a terrible idea because the Christian faith is all about knowing God. Knowing God is where we should begin. So who is this Three-in-One God?

The word "Trinity" isn't found in the Bible but it's the word the church has used for nearly two thousand years to describe God. The word itself may not be there, but the truth that there is one God who exists in three persons is found repeatedly and unmistakeably throughout the pages of scripture.

The Bible says:

1. There is one God.
2. God exists in three distinct persons (Father, Son and Holy Spirit).
3. Each of the three persons is fully God.

There are not multiple gods ruling and reigning over the universe. The God of the Bible is the only God. Isaiah 45:5 says, "I am the LORD, and there is no other; apart from me there is no God." And this one God is Father, Son and Holy Spirit.

In fact, God being Three-in-One is assumed in the Bible. In the same way that most fiction writers don't bother to tell us their characters need to breathe to stay alive, but they sometimes describe people being short of breath, God doesn't say he's Trinity directly but we see this through verses that describe what God's doing. Let me give you some examples.

There are moments when all three persons of God appear together:

> "As soon as **Jesus** was baptised, he went up out of the water. At that moment heaven was opened, and he saw the **Spirit of God** descending like a dove and

> alighting on him. And a **voice from heaven** said, 'This is **my Son**, whom I love; with him I am well pleased.'" (Matthew 3:16–17, emphasis mine)

Jesus taught that when we get baptised, we belong to the Three-in-One God:

> "Therefore go and make disciples of all nations, baptising them in the name of the **Father** ... the **Son**, and ... **Holy Spirit** ..." (Matthew 28:19, emphasis mine)

The disciple Peter talked about God as three distinct persons when he writes to Christians who have been:

> "... chosen according to the foreknowledge of **God the Father**, through the sanctifying work of the **Spirit**, to be obedient to **Jesus Christ** and sprinkled with his blood." (1 Peter 1:2, emphasis mine)

The Apostle Paul signed off his letter to the Corinthian Church by encouraging them that the Three-in-One God is with them:

> "May the grace of the Lord **Jesus Christ**, and the love of **God**, and the fellowship of the **Holy Spirit** be with you all." (2 Corinthians 13:14, emphasis mine)

We can even see something of the persons of God in the very first words of the Bible:

> "In the beginning **God** created the heavens and the earth. Now the earth was formless and empty, darkness was over the surface of the deep, and the **Spirit of God** was hovering over the waters." (Genesis 1:1–2, emphasis mine)

* * *

There's a brilliant moment in Netflix's chart-topping immersive documentary *Drive to Survive,* which follows the lives and careers of the world's best racing drivers. Two of the drivers have been taken by their team to a go-kart track for some publicity photographs. They are told several times not to race each other, and instead to slow down so the photographers can get the shots they need. But they can't do it. It just isn't in their nature! They are racing drivers, and if you put them on a track they'll race each other.

One of them races so hard he ends up crashing off the course altogether, which wasn't the footage the team were after! The drivers just can't help themselves.

What we do always shows who we are, and the same is true with our Three-in-One God. We see God acting towards us in a way that reflects his nature.

The God of the Bible isn't just some solitary figure, happy all alone in heaven. No! The Father, Son and Holy Spirit love one another deeply, and always have. And when God made us, he made us in his image. We are therefore created to be like him. He didn't make us to be alone because he's not alone. He made us for love and friendship and family, and most of all so that we can know *him*.

He made people equal, but he made them different from one another too, again reflecting who he is. God is both absolutely united (one God) and he is beautifully distinct (three persons). The persons of God are distinct and yet wonderfully equal in nature and value. And that's how he's made us too. Being different doesn't mean to be of less worth or value.

Within the fulness of God there is absolute unity and striking equality, so we don't need to fear our differences – whether that's our sex or race or age or personality – we can celebrate them. We can enjoy who God has made us to be, safe in the knowledge that everyone is of equal worth because we are equally made in the image of the Trinity God.

* * *

God is by nature all about putting others first, and so out of the fulness of who he is, he gave the first people Adam and Eve a chance to act like he does: to put him first, by honouring his command. He only gave them one rule and tragically they broke it. And after the first man and woman began to sin there was no way to get the toothpaste back in the tube.

Sin always leads to broken relationships. Everywhere you look, you can see that.

The whole story of the Old Testament is how God faithfully loves his people, despite their unfaithfulness. So eventually, after many generations of patiently giving humans the opportunity to live his way and watching them repeatedly choose to turn their backs on him, God the Father sent his only Son to make a way to restore us. We had disfigured his image within us, and so as Jesus dies on the cross and rises again, he washes us clean and remakes us as new creations, new people, with new hearts. Our relationship with God was fixed.

And that isn't even the whole story! When Jesus ascended to heaven to be with his Father, he didn't abandon us but has left us his Spirit. The Holy Spirit – who comforts us and strengthens us; who convicts us and calls us; who teaches us and transforms us; who empowers us and equips us; who seeks us and keeps us – is with us every single day. He changes our hearts so we can love God and love others.

Paul tells this wonderful story at the start of his letter to the church in Ephesus, and there we learn that before God laid the foundations of the world, his plan was always to save us, through his Son and to give us his Spirit. All of this flows from who God is.

So what?

Now you might be thinking, "Okay fine, I'm going to have to read that over a few times to fully get my head around it, but sure, God is one God, three persons. What difference does that actually make to me? And what does this have to do with my prayers not being answered?"

God being Trinity changes everything when it comes to prayer.

Firstly think about how God is Father. Many of us will have pretty mixed experiences with our dads. Some of us have brilliant dads, others have rubbish dads, some of us have never even met our dads, and tragically some of us have lost our dads. It would be unkind and unwise to assume that everyone has had an easy time with the idea of "Father". But if you've ever been around a family with a really great dad, you'll have an idea about what a father should be.

Little children love to speak to their parents. They just say whatever it is that happens to pop into their heads. Often it's not remotely interesting. Sometimes it's really silly; sometimes it's totally wrong, and yet a good dad turns to them, he smiles, he looks in the child's eyes, and he listens intently. A good dad loves it when his children talk to him.

God is the best Father we can ever imagine and he delights to hear us when we pray. He adores listening to our faltering words. He doesn't worry that we could be saying it better, he just loves to hear our voice. The end goal of prayer isn't ultimately to get what we want, it's to spend time with our Heavenly Father pouring out our thoughts and worries and praise, and in the process learning to get to know him better and depend on him more.

What about God the Son? What difference does he make to prayer? Well the whole reason Jesus came to this world was to make a way for us to know God again, to restore us to friendship with God. Jesus' death, in our place for our sins, means we can know and talk to God. Our prayer life has been bought with a price, and so when we pray we're not just submitting a kind of cosmic shopping list, we're stepping into the freedom we have to approach God Almighty that Jesus won for us on the cross. The very fact that we can pray, that we can speak to the maker of the moon and stars, the King of kings and the Lord of lords is precious beyond belief.

And the Holy Spirit? How does he help us? Well if we trust in Jesus then he gives us his Spirit. It's because of the Holy Spirit that we can be confident that we know God, and it is in the power of the Spirit that we approach the Father in prayer. Romans 8:15 tells us that it's by the Spirit we cry "Abba, Father". By the Spirit we have the power to call God Almighty "Daddy". Jesus makes a way for us to pray, and the Spirit empowers us to do so, and the Father listens intently and delights to hear us when we do.

If we don't get hold of God as Three-in-One, our view of prayer can be a bit like a business deal where we say to God: "Here's what I want, and here's what I'm willing to do to get it!" We've all prayed those sort of prayers haven't we?

- "God if you fix this, I'll never miss church again!"
- "God if you make that person better, I'll never lie again!"
- "God if you let me get off the hook for this, I'll never do it again!"

That isn't prayer really, that's the business of bargaining.

Prayer, at heart, is talking to a God who made us, loves us, saves us, and is with us. Understanding that God is Three-in-One means that whether he chooses to act how we would like to or not, no prayer we ever pray is wasted, forgotten or pointless. We can be sure our Father God hears us because he loves us and Jesus has opened up the way for us. We don't have to promise to do some good deed. We can be sure the Spirit is empowering our prayers and is with us helping and comforting us.

And whether it feels like it or not, God does love to answer our prayers, and we can have faith-filled expectation that he will always answer in the right way (although not always the way we want). He's a good Father who doesn't give a snake to a child when they ask for a snack (see Luke 11:11)!

Now that doesn't mean it's easy when things don't work out the way we would like – of course it isn't! But it does mean that we can trust that God is good, kind, faithful and listening to us when we pray to him. Why not speak to him now? He'd love to listen.

Chapter 3

God is Creator

There is no Planet B.

But when you look at the way the human race acts you might think otherwise. Does it make you angry how little humans seem to care about the damage people are doing to the planet?

Evidence of climate change is becoming more and more obvious every day. As our air becomes increasingly polluted, our water becomes even more contaminated. Sea levels keep rising, extreme weather events are becoming the norm, and many animals are increasingly endangered.

We're destroying our world, polluting our oceans, demolishing our rainforests and no one seems that bothered, do they? I mean, yes there are loud voices saying we must change but the people in the suits making the decisions talk a good game, and deliver very little.

Why doesn't someone do something about it?

And if God is really in charge then why is he letting us do this? Is he bothered about our world? Does he care as much about the environment as I do?

* * *

If you scrolled through my Instagram you'd see that I am hooked on a few different types of accounts. I can't get enough of videos of sausage dogs. They are *way* too cute, and I want to own them all. Then there's the videos of people building handmade acoustic guitars, with levels of artistry I like to imagine Jesus would have been proud of in Joseph's workshop. And then there's the viral nature videos.

I watch people explore places like the Blue Lagoon in Iceland where the mist rises in a perfect cylindrical sheen over the crystal-clear water, bridging the gap between the stunning depths below and the staggering luminescence of the northern lights above.

Then there's the shimmering sands of Tahiti, an island of almost unimaginable beauty that floats alone, enveloped in the blissful peace of the boundless Pacific Ocean. And the Fjords of Norway where sheer cliffs cascade into valleys of the deepest, stillest water and hillsides blaze with the light of a million or more snowflakes, all glistening like tiny diamonds.

I can't get enough of these videos because they give me a tiny window into the scale and beauty of our planet. From the brooding tranquillity of the Scottish lakes, to the untouched explosion of colour found deep in the rainforests, to the mountaintop panoramas of Africa and South America, there is more beauty in our world than we will ever be able to explore. It's astonishing. Breath-taking. Way too big and wonderful to fit in your head.

And here's the most incredible bit of it: God made every single atom.

God is the Creator.

It was all him.

Without him nothing was made that has been made (see John 1:3).

* * *

A while back a really good friend of mine went to see a movie with some mates. She'd had a very long week. She was shattered. Like "don't talk to me, I just need to sit alone and breathe quietly" tired. But her mates dragged her along to the cinema anyway. The problem was the chairs were comfortable, the room was dark and warm, the adverts before the film started were pretty boring and before she knew it, she fell asleep. When she woke up the movie had begun and even though she hadn't missed that much of the runtime, she had slept through several really crucial plot points. She sat there lost in a whole world of sleepy confusion for the next 90+ minutes trying to work out who was who, what was going on, and why any of it even mattered.

It's a bit like that with the story of the Bible. If you miss the beginning, a lot of the rest of it won't make sense. In fact, without Genesis 1–3, it's really hard to get hold of what's going on in the world today. To make sense of who God is and why the world he made is both so beautiful and so broken, we need to start at the very beginning ...

The first two sentences of the Bible show us a huge amount of cosmically important truth:

> "In the beginning God created the heavens and the earth. Now the earth was formless and empty, darkness was over the surface of the deep, and the Spirit of God was hovering over the waters." (Genesis 1:1–2)

God is the main character of the Bible. He's introduced right there in the fourth word. There was nothing before he made the heavens and the earth. There was nothing except God, existing in the perfect unity and endless happiness of the Trinity. God never began. He always was and always is and always will be. Even time can't contain God because he invented it!

The heavens and the earth were not the first thing. God created them. So right in that very first Bible verse we learn that creation didn't come about by chance. It didn't come out of nowhere. In the beginning God was already there and he deliberately, intentionally made the world.

Another of my favourite things to watch on social media are videos of people renovating or building houses (especially tiny ones!). I love their ingenuity and originality, their cleverness and their imagination. I love that process where an idea becomes a reality; where a thought gets made and developed and nailed together – especially when it's packed into a 90-second video!

But as amazing as those people are, they are nothing like God. God didn't pitch up at Ikea, polish off a quick plate of meatballs, grab one of those flatbed trollies, and load up with a car-full of flatpack furnishings. God didn't follow carefully written instructions in order to knock together the heavens and the earth. He didn't upcycle or repurpose things in front of him to make the world. He created from nothing!

He took the formless and empty space and created light and colour and water and sky and plants and vegetation and the sun and moon and stars and birds and, finally, people. He made it all. How? By speaking. *He spoke* creation into being!

He simply said, "Let there be light", and light – which didn't exist before – blazed. Check out Genesis 1 and count how many times "And God said" is repeated. It's a lot!

Creation is utterly mind-blowing. And also immeasurable. But that's not to say some of the cleverest people in the world haven't tried. NASA estimates that the Milky Way – the galaxy we live in – contains approximately 100 billion stars. Now to put that in context, you can fit the earth inside our star, the sun, over a million times. And our galaxy contains 100 billion stars. Roughly.

That's staggering in scale isn't it? But that's only the beginning of it because our galaxy is itself only one of about 100 billion galaxies in the known universe. (Actually 100 billion is a very low estimate, some think it's more like 2 trillion.) And there's bound to be plenty more we don't know about yet.

Doesn't that just blow your mind? Our planet is so big that none of us could ever stand a chance of exploring it all properly in our lifetimes, and it's like a grain of sand on a beach when compared to the rest of our galaxy. And our galaxy is like a grain of sand in the Sahara Desert compared to the rest of the known universe.

And God made it all:

> "By the word of the LORD the heavens were made, their starry host by the breath of his mouth." (Psalm 33:6)

It makes my head hurt just to try to think about it!

* * *

At this point you may be thinking "But what about science? What about the Big Bang? Did God make the world in six 24-hour days?" For some people these are massively significant questions that have a real sway over them. Others don't even really think about them!

I can't address everything here, but imagine you take your favourite pop song to an English teacher and ask them to mark it like a piece of homework. I'm pretty sure it would come back covered in corrections. The grammar would be all over the shop, the infinitives would have been split in all the wrong places, there would be repetition where it isn't needed, and some structural details left out. It wouldn't get a good mark!

But that doesn't mean it isn't a brilliant song. It doesn't even mean it's been badly written. It just means that it isn't trying to be a piece of English language homework.

The account of creation in Genesis 1 is poetic, rhymical and beautiful. It's carefully constructed with shape and form, and when it's read aloud in its original language you can hear the rise and fall and the tempo of the words. It is many things, but at no point does it try to be a scientific textbook explanation of how the world was made. That simply isn't the style of writing we have given to us.

Genesis 1 answers the *who* question of creation: who made the world? God did! It also answers the *why* question. Keep reading for the answer to that! But it doesn't answer the *how* question in precise detail.

I'm not saying for a second that you can't believe that God made the world precisely as Genesis 1 records it; millions of people do and that's totally reasonable. I'm also not saying that you can't take Genesis 1 as a framework to understand how the world was formed. Many have mapped the stages of evolution across the days and found remarkable symmetry and that's totally reasonable too. What is clear is that God is the Creator and his creation shows us more of who he is.

* * *

I was pretty shoddy at art when I was at school. I realised quickly what the problem was. Art takes patience. Beauty comes together slowly. You've got to put the time in, be diligent and delicate, have perseverance and persistence. I didn't have any of that and so I was bad at art. So bad I wasn't even allowed to take it for GCSE whether I wanted to or not – my teacher took the option off the table! That's probably why I hold artists in such high esteem.

When we look at creation, we see that God isn't just a brilliant engineer making a world that works but he's a wonderful artist, creatively making something incredibly beautiful.

Think of the intricate beauty of the Amur leopard as it slowly picks its way through its habitat, the exhilarating power of a lion in full flight; the effortlessness lift of the falcon. Think of the way the coral reefs teem with life and colour; the sounds and the smells of the rainforests; the sight of an open fire or waves breaking on the shore.

Think of the sea turtles as they wiggle and dive; the penguins as they waddle and slide; the whale with thousands of plankton at its side. And don't get me started on sausage dogs …

But of course none of that is even to mention the final piece of God's creation, the crème de la crème, the big finish, the best bit – *people*. Eight billion of us.

Every different height, every distinctive shape and beautiful shade. With bodies of astounding intricacy and sophistication. With minds able to do things that computers never will. With hearts that feel passion and emotion, and that most powerful force of all: love.

We are the reason God made the world. We are the only bit of creation that is labelled "very good", not just because it was a final flourish, but because everything that had come before was building up to that moment. God made the world as a place for people to live in.

We see three reasons people are made in Genesis 1:26–31:

- **To know God's love.** Three times in verses 26 and 27 we're told that people are made in God's image, and it's repeated because it's super important. We are made in the image of a relational God in order that we might have relationship with him. Remember, everything God does flows from his love. He made us to know him and enjoy his love.
- **To care for the world.** In verse 28, God tells the first people they are to rule over the earth. He tells them to care for the world. To look after it. To gently, and patiently labour to make it even more beautiful. To nurture the global garden we live in to bloom into ever greater beauty, Adam and Eve were to be the first gardeners, and all of us since are supposed to have taken up our trowels! Tragically we have done this very badly as a human race. We have not cared for the world as we should have done. We have ruled over it badly.
- **To enjoy God's blessing**. In verse 29, God gives people everything they could ever need: every plant, tree, fruit and vegetable for food, and he gives every creature into their care too. His generosity and provision is incredible! He made us to enjoy his blessings. A massive part of life on this earth is about seeing how good our world is, enjoying it, and thanking God for it! We also

see this on day seven of creation when God rests, setting up a pattern for us. We weren't created just to work, but to stop – finding rest for both our bodies and souls in God.

The problem of course was never with the world God made, but with the choices people have made. The impact of the Fall can be seen all around us in the way we treat this planet today, but there was also another impact back in the Garden of Eden. God cursed the world because of the first gardeners' sin, and all sort of brokenness entered right into the fabric of our planet. Now volcanoes pour out lava on people, earthquakes shatter cities, and tsunamis burst their breakers over beaches and buildings. All the ways our world is wounded, all the ways the beauty is broken, all the ways the planet has been poisoned, it all started with the Fall.

So now the image of God in his world is marred by the brokenness that has infected our planet. But God is still there to be seen, if we look closely. Anything creative reveals something of the person who created it. When you look at a fabulous sketch you see both the picture on the page, and also the spirit of the artist. When you hear a song, you hear the words and the melody, but you also hear the beat of the songwriter's heart. You can't remove who you are from what you make. We put a bit of us in all that we create. And the same is true of God.

Romans 1:20 tells us that God's invisible qualities, his power and his nature can be seen in his creation. Even though broken, what he has made still instructs and informs us of what an amazing Creator he is.

So what?

The state of the environment is one of the most troubling things about life today. It's worrying, and scary, and no one seems bothered.

We seem determined to destroy the only planet that can sustain human life. And we keep making it worse. Every year sea levels rise higher, and pollution gets worse, and nothing seems to change. And it's easy to wonder if God actually cares about the state of the planet.

But knowing God as Creator shows us that *he cares about our world even more than we do*. No matter how deeply you care about the world and the damage we're doing, God cares more. We live here, but this world was his idea.

Perhaps more than any others, those of us who believe in the God of the Bible should strive wholeheartedly to care for our world, because we know the world's Creator and owner. We know he has designed humans to look after it, so we need to do our part!

And that's super challenging, but alongside that we have a hope that is totally irrepressible. This hope keeps bobbing back up to the surface like a beachball pushed under water: God isn't going to let the world be destroyed. The world is precious to God and he's committed to it. Things might get worse but that's not the end of the story. One day Jesus will return and remake our world, and the poison of pollution and plastic will be washed away forever. Like a once sweaty, muddy football kit now washed and aired and good as new, this world will be beautifully renewed. All sin and its consequences will be gone. All the brokenness will be mended.

It's true there's no Planet B, but an upgrade is on its way. In fact, this world might be beautiful now, but we haven't seen anything yet! One day we'll get a front row seat to enjoy Creation 2.0, on a scale and beauty that we can't comprehend.

We'll chuckle and say to one another, "Do you remember how great we used to think those Seven Wonders of the World were? Ha! They would even make the top 100 on the list in this new creation. And you remember those mountains and sunsets – it was like they were in black and white compared to now."

The brokenness we see now will be replaced by a beauty of such brilliance that there will be no contest.

Pollution won't have the last laugh. God has promised us that much!

Chapter 4

God is Different

Loneliness is totally crippling. It saps all your joy and energy and makes you wonder if anyone cares about you at all.

You can sit in the school canteen with a thousand other people and feel totally alone. You can have thousands of contacts at your fingertips and feel like nobody cares.

We can get pretty tired of ourselves too. I know I do.

I feel like I'm a lot to live with. I wind myself up, let alone the people around me. I can be great company, but not all the time. So often a lack of sleep or even just missing a snack and I'm downright foul. I need company but then sometimes I feel awkward around people.

Why do we struggle with ourselves and struggle with others? Why are we so needy?

* * *

It's kind of an obvious thing to say, but God is not like us.

It's so easy to imagine God as just a really, really, really great version of me. Like me on my absolute best day. Like when I've got all my stuff together. But he isn't! He's not the best version of yourself you can imagine. He doesn't think like us, act like us, or live like us. He's different.

Yes, he made us in his image so we resemble him a bit like a self-portrait resembles the artist. But just like paint and canvas are in a different category to a living person, God is in a different category to us altogether. Everything in all of creation goes on one list: Created. God alone sits on another list: Creator.

Imagine one of the streaming giants launches a new reality TV show where contestants must be marooned on a desert island, all alone for weeks on end. And then you discover that one of your mates has nominated you for your chance to win a million pounds for a month spent alone. How would you cope? Does the idea fill you with dread? Would you be bored? If you had no phone for a month would you crumble?

Some of us might quite like the idea of being on our own for a month, but long-term isolation can really damage us. We're just not made for it. In fact solitary confinement is one of the oldest techniques humans have found to break someone's spirit. We don't do well with endless alone time. We're super needy, actually. But God isn't.

God is entirely self-sufficient. He's absolutely independent. But what does that actually mean? Well, this is totally mind-blowing and ever so slightly tricky so you might want to sit up, slap yourself in the face a couple of times, and take a few deep breaths. Ready? Let's go for it.

- **God was always there.** No one made him, created him, caused him or put him there. He just was.

- **God is self-existent.** Nothing gives him life or keeps him alive. He just lives.
- **God is entirely self-reliant.** He doesn't need anyone or anything to help him in anyway. He's never needed anything at all. He has everything he needs in himself.
- **God is absolute.** He cannot be increased or diminished in any way. He is perfect and he always has been and he always will be. He's totally complete.
- **God is constant.** He doesn't get tired, he doesn't go up and down with his moods; he doesn't get hungry or thirsty. His character has always been the same. He's unchanging.
- **God is eternal.** Not only did he never begin, he won't ever end. He's the maker of time itself. He just is.

You might want to read that list again. It's a lot to take in. God is all things at all times, and so needs nothing, ever. Isn't that incredible? He's got it all. Always.

And forgive me for being painfully blunt, but we are nothing like that.

* * *

We are not the cause of ourselves. We grow in our mother's wombs because our parents, well, you know.

And after we're born we're totally helpless, for ages. We can't walk, we can't talk, we can't even sit up. Parents shout it from the rooftops when we learn to roll over, and even then, most of us take a while longer to learn to roll back again. And that most basic human thing of knowing when and how to sleep totally eludes us. We get given wall charts and prizes when we learn to use a toilet. This is not exactly impressive stuff!

Even as teens or adults we're certainly not self-reliant either – we get three minutes without oxygen before we die, three days without water, three weeks without food. From the moment we are born to the time we die we remain astoundingly needy.

We're nothing like complete either, we can always get better, and do better. That's part of why we end up frustrated with ourselves all the time. With literally 8 billion of us on the earth right now, there's always someone able to do something better or faster than we can. And, depending on how you count it, there's been over 100 billion humans alive on our planet at some point, so none of us is exactly unique!

We're certainly not eternal. There was a time when we were not. The planet, the universe and everything was going for a really long time before we came along.

We're definitely not constant. We like to think of ourselves as powerful and strong but if we so much as lose one night of sleep, we're useless. When we haven't seen loved ones we get all stressed and homesick. And if we sit still too long, we actually get more tired. And that's not to mention how illness, disease, or even a cold can wreck our equilibrium. We're crazy needy, all the time.

But God on the other hand …

* * *

God's self-sufficiency is woven through the whole story of scripture. One of the very best places to see it is in Acts 17 where the Apostle Paul is seeking to explain who God is and what he's like to people who don't know him. Paul tells the crowd:

> "The God who made the world and everything in it is the Lord of heaven and earth and does not live in temples built by human hands. And he is not

> served by human hands, as if he needed anything. Rather, he himself gives everyone life and breath and everything else." (Acts 17:24–25)

God doesn't live in human buildings and doesn't rely on people for anything. He doesn't need anything. Instead he himself is the one who provides everything – including life itself. Paul continues:

> "From one man [Adam] he made all the nations, that they should inhabit the whole earth; and he marked out their appointed times in history and the boundaries of their lands." (Acts 17:26)

Remember – around 100 billion people and counting, and he planned out where every single one of us would live. Every nation, and the whole of history, is in his hands.

But Paul's not done:

> "God did this so that they would seek him and perhaps reach out for him and find him, though he is not far from any one of us. 'For in him we live and move and have our being.' As some of your own poets have said, 'We are his offspring.'" (Acts 17:27–28)

Here's where it gets really crazy: read that first sentence in the quote again! We could talk about this sentence for the next 100 years and not scratch the surface of how incredible this is: *the God who needs nothing made us so that we can know him*, and he's not far from any of us. He has no needs, we can't do anything for him, and yet he wants to supply our need for him. He actually wants to know you. He made you in order that you might enjoy knowing him. Forever. That's why you exist, to know and enjoy the God who made you.

* * *

I had a pretty embarrassing experience recently. My colleagues at work organised this lunch that we were all invited to, but I hadn't read the email properly, and so unlike everyone else who turned up with plates of sausage rolls and homemade brownies, I didn't bring anything to share. Even our least enthusiastic staff members had managed to bring some crisps or a bottle of coke but I showed up nothing at all! I felt awful. I felt really guilty. I was eating the food knowing that I'd brought nothing to the table.

Knowing God is like going to this bring-and-share banquet; all 8 billion of us are invited to go along, except none of us brings anything – not so much as a dried-up cheese sandwich – and God brings everything.

There's this amazing moment in Exodus 3 where Moses meets God. At the time Moses was a sheep farmer in the middle of nowhere and came across a bush which was on fire but didn't burn up. Moses thinks it very strange and can't help but wander over to find out more. Suddenly, a voice comes from the bush. It's always called "the burning bush", although if you ask me it's a lot cooler that the bush could talk than that it was on fire, but anyway.

Of course, it's actually God who speaks to Moses in the flames and he sends Moses to lead his people out of slavery in Egypt. When Moses asks who he should say sent him, God answers:

> "This is what you are to say to the Israelites: 'I AM sent me to you.'" (Exodus 3:4)

That's who he is – the great I AM. He just is. No wonder Moses later prayed: "Before the mountains were born, from everlasting to everlasting you are God" (Psalm 90:2).

Revelation 1:8 tells us that God is the Alpha and the Omega, the beginning and the end, who is, and who always was, and who is to come.

* * *

It's worth saying again that God didn't make us because he needed us. He made us to know him. The God who made the world, who needs nothing from you, loves you, for you.

Not for the best version of you, not for the Instagram ideal of you. He loves you for the reality of who you are, complete with the sins you can't shake, and the anxieties and loneliness that are breaking you, and the sadness you feel: he sees all of that and he wants to know you, personally.

What's more, his goodness and his wisdom and his perfection can never be doubted, because unlike us he doesn't have bad days. He isn't affected by others or what's around him. I can have my day ruined by loads of stuff. I can go from being perfectly happy to really upset by one unkind remark, a driver cutting me up, or even a football result that I don't like! I'm like a tent that isn't tied down properly, blown all over the place by the wind. But God isn't anything like that, he's like the strongest reinforced steel building an engineer could ever put together, totally steadfast regardless of what the weather throws at him. Nothing can shake him. Ever.

He doesn't depend on anyone or anything, but he made us to depend on him. *We're actually supposed to depend on him*. When we try to "go it alone" it never works because that was never the idea. In fact, the oldest sin in the world is to turn our backs on God. We're meant to need him, and he's so ready to be needed. He is dependable, generous and has more than enough to meet our every need a million times over.

He only has perfect days, and on every single one of his perfect days he wants you to know him.

So what?

Why does any of that really matter? How does knowing God is different change anything when I feel suffocated by loneliness? How does God's self-sufficiency help me when I'd give anything to have a boyfriend or girlfriend, or even just a friend who gets me? How does God being able to do everything help me, when I feel like I can't do anything and I'm totally overwhelmed?

Well, let's think about it like this. God's independence is like a forcefield around who he is. Nothing can break in and unsettle him. He can't be thrown off course, he can't be thrown up and down by us, or our circumstances, or our world.

He is not remotely needy ever. He has everything he needs, all the time, within himself. And because he doesn't have any needs of his own he's able to help me with mine. And he's able to help you with yours. He actually wants to listen to the prayers of my sinful, feeble, needy mind and grumpy heart. That is beautiful and humbling in the extreme!

So when we're struggling to keep going, we don't need to dig deep to find strength inside us, we can simply ask him for his help. When we're lost in life and don't know which way to go, we don't have to solve it for ourselves, we can ask God to direct us.

When we first leave home and we feel lonely, and a bit ashamed that we'd give anything for a hug we can ask God to draw near. He's ready and waiting. When we aren't happy with ourselves and feel awkward or insecure around others, we can know we don't have to have it all together but we're loved by our maker just the same. When we need someone to understand us, he does.

We have a lot of needs right? I know we're supposed to pretend we don't, but we do. We find ourselves at the end of our abilities all the time. God has never ever experienced that. Instead he is both willing and able to supply all that we could ever need. Why not take some time now to bring your needs to him in prayer? We can be confident that he is listening and able to help.

Chapter 5

God is Holy

The world is so messed up. We can agree on that right?

You can't watch the news without hearing about something awful happening somewhere. Why are people like this? And how is it that this stuff has become so normalised that we don't even blink at it anymore? There's always war somewhere! Whether it's open warfare in Europe, ancient conflicts that don't seem to end in the Middle East, fighting over territory in Africa, or civil wars in South America; one nation or organisation constantly seems to be bombing another.

No one can sort it out. Certainly not world leaders. Everyone only seems to be in it for what they can get. The politicians who peer out over their podiums seem to love nothing more than projecting their power. The same hands that wave to their adoring voters hover over nuclear missile launch buttons. How can we trust those running the show when so many world leaders act like a bunch of stroppy toddlers who might just lose it and tear the walls down. It's scary right? However bad it is today, we're only ever a couple of bruised egos away from things getting even worse.

Do you ever look at it all and wonder what on earth we're doing as humans? Why we seem so continuously committed to violence and bloodshed? And where on earth does God fit into all of this?

* * *

When I was growing up, I got in trouble quite a lot. I mean, I deserved it. My parents were brilliant but I wasn't always a joy to be around. My behaviour was so bad at one stage they almost expelled me from Sunday school and those were some patient people leading that group!

The problem was, I had so many great ideas. Or what I thought were great ideas. Practising amazing new football skills led to smashed windows. I enjoyed winding people up and I had a problem with making smart comments, or at least they felt clever at the time. One double GCSE graphics lesson I came really unstuck. My long-suffering teacher paused sadly as he looked at my work, shook his head and said: "Acheson, you really can't draw." I replied far too quickly with: "Sir, you really can't teach." I deserved the punishment I got for that.

But my big sister never got into trouble. Ever. Coralie was perfect; sooooo annoyingly good. She was polite, kind, hardworking, brilliant at school. I don't think she ever broke a cup, let alone a window.

I did all sorts wrong but not Coralie. No, she behaved beautifully.

Or so it seemed. But of course she wasn't actually flawless. She messed up too, and looking back now I can see that, even though I couldn't at the time. She wasn't really perfect.

But God is. He really is. Or to put it another way: God is holy.

God has never and will never get anything wrong, to any extent. He doesn't sin. At all. In fact, he can't. Why? Because holiness isn't something he does, it's something he is.

Just like a fish can't wake up one morning (I'm not actually sure if fish do wake up in the morning, but I imagine they do) and just decide, do you know what? I'm done with all this swimming. I'm over it. I'm bored of this "two hydrogens, one oxygen" molecular structure in which I spend all my days. I'm going to be a flying creature from now on. I'm moving on up!

To state the obvious, a fish can't fly like a bird. That's not who he is – the fish has to swim by definition. God is without sin by definition. He won't ever get anything wrong because it isn't in his nature. He is goodness, and he's always pure throughout every fibre of his being. God is light and in him there is no darkness at all (1 John 1:5).

And I know this is again obvious, but we are not like that. We can't manage a day of being holy, whereas he's done that and will do that for eternity. Most of us can't manage an hour, especially when we're hungry.

We are the opposite of holy: we're broken! We're sinners! And it's not just when we choose to do stuff we know we shouldn't do; it's deeper than that, it's actually in our nature. There's something about being a human that means sinfulness is woven into us. It's a part of the package deal. Like the charging cable that we get in the box when we buy a new phone, it all comes together.

We reject God by our choices *and* by our nature, just like our ancestors Adam and Eve before us. We've inherited their problem of thinking we know better than God, and so in our deeds and our hearts we don't live his way. We've all got the ability to hurt others. Every human does. And the more power we have, the more damage we can do. This means that the root cause of all the wars in the world isn't the politics or the circumstances we find ourselves in, it's the sin in our human hearts.

Even on our absolute best day, we fall short. Romans 3:23 tells us that all have sinned and fallen short of the glory of God. We don't measure up to his matchless perfection and holiness.

"If we claim to be without sin, we deceive ourselves and the truth is not in us" (1 John 1:8). We can kid ourselves if we want, but we're only fooling ourselves, we're not fooling anyone else, and certainly not God. We'd all like to claim that we've lived our lives with no regrets, but that's not actually true for any of us deep down. We've all got stacks of regrets. We've all got loads of things that we've said and we've done that we would love to undo. I know I do.

* * *

Have you ever asked yourself the same question like fifteen times? It's normally because the answer is really important, like when you ask yourself "Where's my ticket?" on the way to a concert. We ask it as we leave the house, double-checking it definitely is in our pocket. Again we're asking and checking when we get to the train station, again in the queue for the venue. We repeat ourselves when stuff really matters. The same is true in the Bible.

The angels in Isaiah 6 call out to one another "Holy, holy, holy is the LORD Almighty" and they don't repeat themselves for the sake of it. Saying the Lord is holy once isn't enough, and even twice won't cut it. They say it three times. Like God is holy cubed! This is actually the strongest possible way the Hebrew language can say something. God is holy three times over!

It's the very same song that all of creation sings around the throne of God in Revelation 4:8: "'Holy, holy, holy is the Lord God Almighty' who was, and is, and is to come." He is spotless, without a single shadow; he never wavers or wanders. This should be a source of immense encouragement to us as we live in this tragic, dark, broken world. God isn't infected with the same sin disease like the rest of us. Praise God that he is holy! In a world where there is so much evil and sin he remains steadfast and he always will.

* * *

But whereas God will never change, the good news is that we will. If we trust in Jesus and seek to follow God's ways and God's Word in our lives he doesn't leave us as we are. He's committed to making us holy too. He does that by the work of his Holy Spirit in us, changing us more into his likeness.

So all the stuff in my heart that I'm ashamed of and wish wasn't there, and all the stuff in you that you wish wasn't there – all that sin you can't shake – doesn't need to cause you despair. It doesn't make you useless or a lost cause. Why? Because God himself is working within you to make you more like him. To make you holy as he is holy.

Every day, if we know God, his Spirit is working within us to make us more like Jesus, and one day we will be totally without sin. One day we will actually be fully holy, when we are with Jesus in glory.

Imagine someone who's really out of shape joins a gym. Like really, really out of shape. They start eating right and working out, and slowly they begin to make some tiny progress. That's pretty great. But imagine you were able to show them a portrait of themselves in the future where they are in perfect shape. Not a single gram of fat anywhere to be found, beautifully proportioned and toned muscles, a stunning beach-ready six-pack and arms a boxer would be proud of. It would almost feel too good to be true, when they are so far from that now.

Of course there's no guarantees from a gym membership, but we can be sure God is going to make us perfectly holy. If we trust Jesus, there is a day coming for us when sin will be a distant memory.

So does that mean sin doesn't really matter today? Does it mean God isn't bothered about it now? No! God takes sin really seriously. He is holy after all!

He takes our sin so seriously that he sent his own Son to die for us. The wages of sin is death and the price had to be paid. As Jesus hung on that splintering wooden cross he paid the price for the sin of all those who trust in him.

Without his perfect holiness, he couldn't save me. He couldn't save you either. If God is just as messed up as me, then he's no help to me sorting out my brokenness and sin. But he isn't. Jesus came to this earth and lived a spotless perfect life on our behalf. We now have nothing to fear from the holiness of God because Jesus, God's Son, has given us his holiness when he saved us, and God's Spirit is at work in us even now making us more like Jesus, if we trust in him.

So what?

God isn't like us. He's completely holy, all the time. But how does that work when the world he has made is in such a state? What does his holiness mean to a world where wars keep starting? What about the bombs and the bullets and the blades? How can we be sure he is so holy after all? He might have started off good but how do we know that God isn't just like any other human leader corrupted by their own power?

Remember, knowing who God is and what he is like helps us understand why he acts the way he does in the world. We can't allow what we see with our eyes to affect our view of God, rather we must allow our view of God to shape how we see the events of our world.

In his goodness, God has allowed the people he created the freedom to choose how they act. And humanity has consistently chosen to hurt and to harm one another, and we are still doing that. God stands apart from all this evil, but that doesn't mean he's absent from the world he made. Even in the mess, he is always working in the world. He never stops working for the good of those who love him, making us more like Jesus (Romans 8:28–29). If we're Christians, no war or persecution or disaster can separate us from his love. His love is everywhere and we can't escape it, no matter what happens (Romans 8:35–39). He's growing his church around the world, he's saving people and changing people every day.

He's also being patient. He's giving people time to repent and turn to him before Judgement Day (2 Peter 3:9).

But that doesn't make him weak. He won't wait forever. God is a God of justice and he will not allow the evil in our world to go unchecked. He has chosen a day in the future when Jesus will return and every wrong will be made right (Acts 17:30–1). Every knee will bow before him (Philippians 2:10). God cannot and will not ignore evil. Every war will stop, every evil will be punished and God will rule in perfect peace. Justice will be done because God is holy.

But this isn't just a global scale thing, it's personal too. God's justice means he won't put up with the evil in us either. Which might seem frightening. The twin realities of our sin and God's justice seem to put us on a collision course. God takes both justice and the evil that we have done incredibly seriously. Our sin hurts us and grieves God. But this is where we meet with the glorious hope of the gospel once again. Our sin is so serious that it led Jesus to the cross. Jesus offers us free and full forgiveness forever. Jesus fixes and forgives all our failings when we reject our sin and turn to him instead. And what's more, he gifts us his holiness, and calls us to walk in holiness and seek each day to turn away from sin; to be holy as he is holy (1 Peter 1:16).

God isn't like every other failed leader we've experienced or heard of. He's unfaltering. He's a leader who will never change his mind. He will never leave or forsake his people. He will never resign amidst scandal. He'll never need to retire. He'll never become corrupt. He'll never forget you. More than that he is saving and changing people.

He's holy. He always will be. And as we look at our world we see that that is very good news indeed. But I guess the question for some reading this is, if you're not a Christian, are you willing to let God be the leader of your life? Are you willing to trust in Jesus' holiness in the face of God's perfect judgement?

Chapter 6

God is Sovereign

Technology is moving so fast that it's hard for humans to keep up. Your grandparents probably grew up with a phone attached to the wall in their hallway, now it's almost like we all have access to J.A.R.V.I.S. from *Iron Man* in our pocket.

Internet AI is amazing in its power and ability, but it hasn't taken long before it's started to feel a little bit sinister too. Musicians have begun to campaign against the dangers of AI in the music industry. Deep Fakes are everywhere, and they are really convincing. "AI stole my face" is something we're hearing said more and more. You could get a video call from someone who looks like your mum or dad chatting away to you, asking you do certain things and it might not be them at all. Governments have caught terrorists trying to use AI to mount chemical attacks, and we're all totally accustomed to hackers breaking into our online spaces.

AI is very cool, and really scary. The most frightening thing about it is that no one seems to be able to get hold of it. It's growing at a speed and scale that even tech experts are shocked by, and this is just the start. Maybe all those movies about robots taking over the world weren't quite so crazy after all.

The internet, and social media in particular, is a lawless place – a kind of Wild West where everyone is out for themselves, and you need to watch your back because no one else will. Technology has an appetite which seems impossible to satisfy, a thirst that's impossible to quench. It always seems to be hungry for more of our lives doesn't it? Wanting to take up more and more of our bandwidth, for us to live more and more digitally and less and less physically. Being committed to face-to-face interaction feels pretty revolutionary and it seems like it's harder to keep anything private anymore, which is stressful and tiring. No wonder we're exhausted by the growing demands of the devices that live in our pockets, in our palms and on our wrists.

* * *

I love some of those old movies that tried to imagine what the future would look like. Famously *Back to the Future II* transported Marty McFly from 1985 to 2015. Filmed in the late 80s, the movie imagined a world with flying cars and hovering skate boards. It's worth watching a clip on YouTube! Most science fiction predications have been so wrong that they're funny, but the rapid growth in AI in the last few years has been greater than anyone could have guessed.

Want a video of a monkey riding on a camel singing the national anthem on a snowy night? AI can do that for you. Want an image in the style of Van Gogh of seventeen piglets flossing? No problem. Need a 2,000-word essay on the complicated relationship between spaghetti and bolognaise in Europe over the last 500 years with reference to grated cheese? Takes seconds. I could probably have asked it to write this book for me, and it might have done a better job!

AI is really something, but it's nothing compared to God.

AI might be big, but God is sovereign. Totally in charge. That's the word the Bible uses to explain this, and it's the most brilliant news. In this chapter we'll see that the antidote to AI anxiety is the authority of the Almighty.

What does it mean that God is sovereign? Let's put it really simply. I'll even give you a little trick to remember it. Make a fist, and then say the next five words out loud, and starting with your thumb release a digit for each word, ready? Okay.

> "God rules everything everywhere always."

There is nothing anywhere ever that he is not in charge of. So you can think of anything, and whatever it is, whenever it is, God rules over it. The rate grass grows in my garden? He decides. Tomorrow's news? Yep. The history syllabus in school? Absolutely.

No matter how big or small, scary or exciting, wonderful or heart-breaking, God rules over it. There is no place on this planet, or space in our society, digital or physical where God is not in charge.

The prophets in the Old Testament loved to call him the "Sovereign LORD" and the Bible finds ways to tell us over and over again that God reigns supreme. Psalm 103:19 says: "The Lord has established his throne in the heavens, and his kingdom rules over all."

Confused and perplexed about what God is doing on one occasion, the prophet Jeremiah still prays: "Sovereign Lord, you have made the heavens and the earth by your great power and outstretched arm. Nothing is too hard for you" (Jeremiah 32:17).

Jesus tells his disciples that with God all things are possible (Matthew 19:26). Why? Because God is sovereign, ruling and reigning over everything, always. And whether or not someone chooses to believe that doesn't change the reality of it one little bit. I could choose not to believe in gravity right now, but it wouldn't change the result as I leapt off the diving board at the swimming pool. The most fundamental rule in the universe, far beyond anything science has decided or discovered is that there is a God and he is in charge. He made everything, he owns everything, and he rules everything.

But it's not like God gets out of bed every morning and says: "I think it's going to be one of those days where I choose to be in charge of every atom and particle, molecule and follicle in the universe, and then I'll kick back later with a massive bar of chocolate and a movie." No, being sovereign isn't something God switches on or off, it's who he is in his very nature.

But, here's the thing. You might be reading that and thinking, wow, that's a lot to take in. But even if I do accept it, even if I do believe that there's a God and he's sovereignly ruling and reigning … why is that a good thing?

How is that any better than saying technology is in charge? It kind of feels like the same thing: some distant uncontrollable power gets to decide everything in my life, and I just have to accept that. Like being stuck on a delayed and redirected train, I don't get a say in where I'm going. Only this isn't a train, it's my life, my friends, my family, my health, my relationships, me. I just get carried along while someone else calls the shots.

And do I even want God calling the shots? I mean there's plenty of stuff in the world that he doesn't seem to be doing a very good job with. Just take the internet for one example. Why is social media so full of trolling and pain? Why are children groomed online? Why does porn get to be so prominent and destructive to our view of relationships? Why do so many people end up trafficked and abused to feed the porn industry? Where are you God? If you really are sovereign why do you allow humans to mess up the world you made so badly? What's the deal with that?

* * *

Whether our struggles are online or offline, they are often incredibly painful and personal. And when we hear God is sovereign and in control of these things, it can make him feel more distant and uncaring than ever. If you feel that way, I totally get that. But God isn't far away or fickle. The reason God spoke this world into existence in the first place was to create a place for the people he wanted to make and to love. And the reason he can guarantee he will always be with us, helping us and actively loving us, is that he is sovereign. Nothing is outside his control, so nothing can stop him being close to us and acting for good in our lives.

Romans 8:28 says: "And we know that God causes everything to work together for the good of those who love God and are called according to his purpose for them" (NLT). God sovereignly works for the good of those who love him *in all things*. Not some things, not most things, but in all things, if we know and trust the Lord Jesus. The God who rules and reigns is out for your good. He wants the best for you, every single second of every single day if you trust in Jesus.

Granted, it doesn't always feel like this, but imagine with me a child that just wants to eat ice cream all day, every day. Let's call him Ben. Or Jerry. Doesn't matter. This kid loves that frozen cream. Chocolate, vanilla, thunder and lightning ... He even likes toothpaste-flavoured ice cream – some people might call it mint choc chip – which is completely disgusting. If his parents would let him, he'd eat it by the bucketload. But they don't. You should just hear his weeping and wailing when they say "no more". He doesn't understand how his parents could be so mean. But they are in charge and they decide how much he gets to eat. They use their power and authority for their son's good even when he doesn't understand.

We often want to tell God that *we* know best and that he should give us what *we* want. Of course, our problems are bigger than wanting more ice cream but God still knows what he's doing in our lives.

Remember the God who made, owns, knows and rules all things is out for your good. But he might have a different type of good in mind for you than you do:

> "And we know that God causes everything to work together for the good of those who love God and are called according to his purpose for them. For God knew his people in advance, and he chose them to become like his Son …" (Romans 8:28–29, NLT)

In every situation God is working to make us more like Jesus. Not to give us all the things we want or even to always take our suffering away, but to shape our characters to be like his Son. Just like a good personal trainer makes us feel pain in the process of getting us in shape, being conformed into Christ's likeness will not be without effort and cost. But God is committed to your good all the time, no matter how it feels.

Working for our good is not the only thing God is sovereignly doing in the world however …

* * *

One classic answer to the question "What's the purpose of humans?" begins: "to glorify God".[1] God, in his sovereignty, has made us to bring him glory, and he is sovereignly working in us to help us do that.

Time and again in the Bible we read that God is at work for his glory in the world. For example, in Isaiah 48:11 God says: "I will not yield my glory to another." God tells us in Isaiah 43:7 that he has made us for his glory. In Psalm 29:2, we're told to give God "the glory due to his name".

And if you're reading this and thinking: "I'm really not sure why you'd think that's a good thing!", I hear you. It's easy to get a bit uncomfortable at this point. Suddenly God sounds like a headteacher lining up Year 7 and telling them how fortunate they are to have a headteacher like her. They'd think she was crazy! Especially if she was some terrible Trunchbull-like tyrant who just used her power to intimidate others. Why should she force her pupils to slave away just so that she can look brilliant to the school inspectors? Humans – especially those who have some power – are often out for their own glory and it's never good for anyone else.

1 See The Westminster Shorter Catechism, Question 1.

But God isn't like us. He isn't on a power trip. We usually talk about glory meaning fame or acclaim or respect, like we rightly give glory to those who achieve amazing things. We should certainly give God honour and seek to make him known, but God's glory means so much more than that. He is glorious regardless of what people think of him.

God's glory literally means who he is.

The most commonly used word for glory in the Bible comes from the Hebrew word *kavod* which literally means weight or heaviness. It means the full weight, or the totality, of something. So God's glory is about the wholeness of his being, the fulness of who he is. God's glory is shorthand for saying that God is everything that we know that he is.

So God's radiant glory is shown by his power, by the world he has made, by the beauty we see all around us. The heavens declare his glory (Psalm 19:1). We see God's glory when he answers prayer, when we feel his presence, when we hear his voice in his Word. We experience his glory in different ways, but each one of those ways by itself doesn't capture his glory – it merely gives us a hint.

God's glory means his kindness, love, compassion, mercy, grace, majesty, strength, authority, power, gentleness, patience, meekness, self-sufficiency, humility and holiness. The totality of God is the glory of God.

So we might read the idea that God uses his sovereignty to work for his glory and think that's bad news for us, but it's actually unbelievably brilliant news for us. Think about it.

If the God who is good and kind and just and merciful and faithful and wise and holy is the one who makes all the plans, those plans will be good and kind and just and merciful and faithful and wise and holy. In other words, they will be really, really great plans. Great for him *and* for us too. Imagine you're about to throw a party and the best party planner in the world offers to come and organise it for you? You'd be delighted to hand them the reins!

The classic answer to the question I mentioned earlier – "What's the purpose of humans?" – begins: "to glorify God" and then it continues: "and to enjoy him forever". For Christians, God's glory and our happiness come as a package deal. And the fact he's in control guarantees the outcome. We can trust his sovereign plans because they are for our good and his glory, everything perfectly in line with his loving, gracious, just heart. So it's win-win.

One of my favourite Bible stories is the book of Esther. It's about this unbelievably powerful King called Xerxes and an evil plot from his right-hand man Haman to destroy all of God's people. At first glance it looks like God is nowhere to be found – he isn't even mentioned in the book. But his hidden hand is at work in every moment. Like a master choreographer who decides which move comes next, God places Esther right where she needs to be so God's people are saved. Even though it looks like God's absent most of the time, he's always in full control – and that's how it is in our world too.

When Jesus comes back, he is going to fix everything forever. And it will then all make sense. We'll realise he knew what he was doing in every moment, and that his plans were always perfect.

So what?

Technology seems to be getting more and more powerful all the time and it's a bit frightening. But when we get anxious about AI taking over, the answer isn't to throw our phones off a cliff and go and live in a cave. That won't give us lasting peace in an increasingly digital world. (Although cutting down our phone use might help a bit!) The solution to the stress we find in the wake of the ever-advancing technology that gives computers more and more power and human-like thinking abilities isn't to flee from technology, but to rest in who God is. He's in charge. Really, he is.

He rules over the internet and AI. When it feels like the world is out of control and the bots have taken over we need not fear, God's in charge. When the deep fakes make us wonder how to know what is true, we can go to God's Word, the Bible, and trust that even if everyone else is a liar, God isn't.

I hate the phrase "you've got this". Because to be honest whatever it is, I almost always haven't got it. I'm a mess. I forget things, and I get stuff wrong a lot. I haven't got this. But God's sovereignty means that he *has* got this. Whatever it is. God's got it. Forever.

God is sovereign and that is wonderful, can't-stop-yourself-smiling, brilliantly good news.

Chapter 7

God is Jealous

Anxiety is horrible isn't it? Worse than horrible. Suffocating and dominating. That nagging, stressful tension that sort of sits really deep down inside us, and at the same time feels like it's right on the surface ready to explode at any moment. It's the creeping feeling of dread; sometimes like everything is moving way too fast, or way too slow. It can feel like everyone is looking at you even when they're not. Cold sweats, tears, dizziness. Knowing that you've lost perspective, but not being able to ground yourself anywhere to find some. There's an edginess to it, a breathlessness to it, a I've-just-gotta-get-out-of-here-right-now-or-I'll-scream thing about it. It's exhausting, taking all your joy and your appetite away. It's really isolating and lonely, even when you're in a crowd. Anxiety sucks.

If you're reading this and a lot of it is ringing true with you, you must talk to someone about it – a trusted friend, a parent, someone at church who cares about you. Let them in on what you're feeling (put in a text if a conversation feels too much). I'd encourage you to see a doctor if you're experiencing physical symptoms. Talking will help.

We get anxious about so many things: friendships, social gatherings, crowds, results, money, purpose, relationships …

One of the biggest reasons we get anxious is when we worry about what people think of us.

A lot of our anxiety surrounds identity. We don't really know who we are, or where we fit, or how to fit, and so we end up really fearful of what other people think of us. And some of us don't just worry about what *people* think of us, we also worry about what *God thinks* of us. After all, he hears all those little lies and horrible thoughts, he sees what we look at on our phone, he knows all our failures and weaknesses.

No wonder we feel crushed with anxiety.

* * *

When people ask me where I'm from, I never really know what the answer is. I was born in Zimbabwe, my family are from Northern Ireland and I've spent most of my life living all over the place in England.

When I was a kid, every summer we'd spend a few weeks of the school holidays with grandparents, aunts and uncles in Northern Ireland. I loved it. My parents have always called it home. I spent a gap year there too, getting to know some of my very favourite people. I still try and go over every year to see family and friends. And something really strange happens to me when I arrive – and it's just about the only time I feel like this – I start to feel this lovely warm feeling, like I just fit.

My accent is all wrong and I'm really English in lots of ways, but when I get off the boat or step off the plane, there's this hard-to-wrap-words-around buzz. Somehow I'm safe. Somehow I belong. I feel this quiet ease. It's relaxing, peaceful and a bit euphoric all at the same time. You might get something similar when you come home from uni. It's a "belonging".

In the deepest corners of our hearts, we yearn to belong. More than anything else, we all long for home, to find ourselves where we are accepted and loved. There's something written into our DNA – hardwired into our souls – that tells us that we find out who we really are when we know who loves us. The centre of our identity is always located in where we belong.

The problem is we can spend all our lives pursuing this life-defining love, trying to fill the hole in our souls, seeking to quench our thirst to belong, but we end up more thirsty than ever when the people we thought loved us let us down. And even if we have great parents and friends, it still doesn't always seem enough.

The reality is that we can only ever find the fulness of our identity in knowing God's love. We rest, when we rest in him. He is the one who loves us more than any other person has, can, or ever will. If we're trusting in him, we know that he not only made us and sustains us, but he sent his Son Jesus to find us and save us. His love for his children is intense, powerful, vibrant and explosive.

God is jealous in his love, and that is excellent news.

* * *

Let's address the elephant in the room first: jealousy sounds like a really bad thing doesn't it? I mean saying God is love, that's great; but saying that God is jealous …? That doesn't sound good at all. A jealous boyfriend is suffocating and a jealous friend is exhausting; even a jealous pet is annoying. Who would want a jealous God?

We read verses like Exodus 34:14 which says: "Do not worship any other god, for the LORD, whose name is Jealous, is a jealous God", and it's easy to feel super uncomfortable. God sounds overbearing, maybe even a bit controlling. It's hard to know what to do with a verse like that.

Or what about Zechariah 8:2: "This is what the LORD Almighty says: 'I am very jealous for Zion; I am burning with jealousy for her.'" Is it okay that God speaks about his people like this? Feels a bit awkward. We don't really like the idea that God is jealous very much.

That's understandable. We see jealousy as a bad thing because it normally is. Often when people get jealous they get controlling and possessive and unkind. Jealously leads people into all sorts of bad places. In the Bible when Joseph's brothers get jealous of him, that nearly leads them to murder. They kidnap Joseph, sell him into slavery and then lie to cover up their sin.

Human jealously is often wrong. But not always.

Imagine a young man who has been hopelessly, tragically in love with a girl he's known for years. She's beautiful. Her eyes light up the room, and she moves with this energy and grace that he finds almost overpowering. Intoxicating. Overwhelming. He has to concentrate hard to stop himself just staring at her when they're together. He just wants to be around her. Then incredibly he starts to suspect that she might like him back. He catches her smiling at him; she starts to seek him out. They laugh together, walk together, and eventually get together. He's ecstatic.

As time passes they are engaged and then one bright summer's day he sees her walk up the aisle in white and hears her make those incredible wedding vows: forsaking all others she commits herself completely to him. All his dreams have come to pass.

But then imagine one day he discovers his wife is in danger. There's someone stalking her, sending her menacing letters and threatening to hurt her. How would he react? Would anything be able to stop his burning love for her?

When it comes to God's jealousy, don't think of the controlling teen who won't let his girlfriend so much as talk to another boy. Think of the husband who would give everything to protect his bride.

* * *

Jealousy differs from envy, which is all about wanting something that doesn't belong to you; something that you don't have any right to anyway. Instead, jealousy is that thing that erupts inside when someone tries to take something that's precious to you, or when someone tries to give something of yours to someone else.

The Hebrew word in the Bible that often gets translated "jealous" in the Old Testament is *qana'* and is used when God's people are choosing to turn their backs on him and give their hearts to other gods which will corrupt and ruin them. *Qana'* describes a love that won't let go, that gets provoked to anger and passion when God's people are in danger of destruction. God's jealousy is a consuming fire. With the intensity of a dragon guarding her eggs or a mother bear protecting her cubs, God's love is of such stratospheric strength and purity that it scorches those who seek to tarnish it.

God's jealous love is more powerful than we can imagine. It's eternal and it won't ever stop. It's all-consuming, nothing can stand in its path. But the most astonishing thing about the jealous love of God is not its power (although God does have all the power), it's not its longevity (it never dies, but then the same is true of God), it's not even its intensity – no, the most incredible thing about the jealous love of God is its *direction*. The thing God so jealously protects, the concentration of his burning affection is … his people. It's us. It's his church. If you believe and trust in him, it's you.

Imagine a parent whose child is kidnapped. A dad who has lost his little boy and fears he may never see him again. Imagine that dad is also the police officer heading up the search. Imagine the intensity of the jealous love of that parent as he chases down leads and hunts down the kidnapper. Imagine the force of his desire to save his child. Imagine the fire burning in his eyes as he does everything he can to find his son. Can you imagine anything stronger? I doubt it.

Jealous love is just about the most powerful force this world knows.

When we become Christians, we become God's children and he protects us like the best Father. You'll never be able to comprehend how enormous God's love is for you. It's astounding in power, beauty and glory.

He loves you so much that he's jealous for you.

* * *

Let's go back to those verses we began with and read them rightly:

> "Do not worship any other god, for the LORD, whose name is Jealous, is a jealous God."(Exodus 34:14)

> "This is what the LORD Almighty says: 'I am very jealous for Zion; I am burning with jealousy for her.'" (Zechariah 8:2)

Do you see how much God loves his people? Do you see the extent of his passionate love for them? He *burns* for them. It's remarkable to think that the God who made all things, knows all things, owns all things and rules all things, loves his people – you! – like this. He doesn't want them to give their hearts to any other god but him.

We were made for him, and worshipping any other god is therefore sinful and, to put it simply, really bad for us. False worship is like a disease in our souls, eating away at us, and God wants to heal us.

Imagine a cancer surgeon operating on her best friend. They've been best friends for years. The two girls grew up together. As children they got in trouble together when they came in too late from playing at night. They commiserated over break-ups with buckets of ice cream in their teens. They went to uni together, were bridesmaids for each other, shared parenting tips and went on holidays together. They've prayed together, laughed together, and cried together through the ups and downs of life.

And now the surgeon's best friend has been tragically diagnosed with this awful illness. Thankfully it is not too late and the cancer can still be cut away. Imagine the diligence, patience, passion, concentration of that friend as she meticulously, beautifully, inexhaustibly works until every last sinew of disease is cut away;

jealously destroying the damaged cells until every last one is gone.

Our souls are only healthy when our hearts are worshipping God. God is jealous for our worship. He wants us to give him the honour only he is due. He wants us to look to him for meaning, purpose and direction and not find those things anywhere else.

Meeting together as a church is certainly an important and special part of this, but worship is more than singing. Romans 12:1 really helps us understand what worship is all about:

> "Therefore, I urge you, brothers and sisters, in view of God's mercy, to offer your bodies as a living sacrifice, holy and pleasing to God – this is your true and proper worship."

True and proper worship means giving our whole bodies, all the time. We give ourselves to God because Jesus gave all he had for us on the cross – that's the mercy mentioned here. It's in light of God's generosity to us that we worship him in return. We should honour him with our money, with our relationships, with our time, with the way we act online, in prayer, in song, in everything. He doesn't want us to put anything before him, he doesn't want us to listen to anyone above him, or love anyone more than him.

If that sounds like a lot, even a bit too much, then just imagine if God wasn't jealous for our worship. What if he couldn't care less about how we lived? If he didn't care about our hearts getting broken and so just let us sleep around and make sex our most important thing. Imagine if he didn't want our love and wasn't bothered about us at all – not lifting a finger to save us or bring us into his family. Like an absent parent who has no idea what we're into or up to, it would be terrible if he was totally disinterested in our lives. It's a brilliant thing that God is jealous for our worship.

He's jealous for us because he wants what is best for us. He's knows us better than we even know ourselves and he wants us to find life, and life to the full (John 10:10). He knows how we can do that and longs that we will be full of his love in our lives. He wants us to be filled with his Spirit (James 4:5), and therefore be full of the fruit of his Spirit (Galatians 5:22–23).

And he knows that if we look for life and hope and meaning and purpose anywhere else, it will be like drinking from a broken, dry, dusty bowl rather than a fountain of pure spring water (Jeremiah 2:13). Only when we give him our worship will we find our fulfilment. He wants us to know true blessedness, true happiness, and we can only find that in him.

So what?

Anxiety is everywhere, and it's totally debilitating. We're paralysed by what people think of us, so we don't put ourselves out there or try and join in with things or go to that party we'd love to be at, and we miss out. A lot of the time our anxiety comes from a place of insecurity, of being unsure of our identity, of who we are and how we belong.

It's like that for Anxious Alice as she sits at the bottom of the stairs, folding her fingers and tapping her toes, terrified about what Made-up Mia might have been saying behind her back and how her Hypothetical Head of Year will react when she doesn't hand in her homework.

Or Stressy Stew, frantically bouncing on the balls of his feet, as he stands waiting for the bus to college, knowing everyone expects so much of him and has such high hopes for his future. What if he can't keep up? What if he lets everyone down? If he's not top of his class, then who is he?

The truth is that all of us find the deepest reality of our identity in knowing that we are loved, and we can never be fully fulfilled until we know God's love in our lives. It won't come even if everyone else likes us or we succeed in every area of life. There's a hole in souls only knowing God can fill. But wonderfully God loves us. And he doesn't just love us a little bit. He loves us with inexhaustible, stunning, endless, burning, jealous love.

God loves us so much he is jealous for us. So whatever Anxious Alice or Stressy Stew or me or you have coming up today, we can find our safe ground – our equilibrium, that sweet sense of belonging, that warmth of home – by resting in the love of God.

The ultimate antidote to our anxiety is to know the jealous love of God in our lives. He couldn't love you anymore than he does already. Hallelujah!

Chapter 8

God is Simple

We've covered a lot of ground so far – thanks for sticking with me – and the things we've looked at about God have been really incredible. God is astonishing in his "God-ness"! But even if we know in our *heads* that he is a loving, holy Creator, who cares for us and rules for our good, why doesn't it always *feel* like that? Why is what I see in my life so out of sync with what I read in his Word?

Can we just let our guard down and be real about this for a minute: Sometimes it's like God's gone; like he's a million miles away. He appears angry or absent. He's supposed to be with us and yet we feel totally on our own. One day it feels like he hears our prayers, another day it's like we're talking to the ceiling. Sometimes we have that warm sensation that says "God's got me", other days he does nothing to lift our sadness.

We look to the Bible for reassurance and on one page we find a God who becomes a little baby born in a stable and on another page a God who slays his enemies, turns people into pillars of salt, and sends down fire upon whole cities! Sometimes he's full of power, terror and vengeance, and other times he's a portrait of mercy, kindness and humility. No wonder we never know where we are with him! We can be real about that right?

Is God like one of those famous people who we all thought was lovely until we discover that he's actually just a brutal bully with a fake smile? Can we really claim that God is all of the things this book has said he is, when he seems to be so inconsistent?

* * *

Christmas tends to be the time when all the worst cake comes out. It's a scandal every year that – in the joy and excitement of Christmas – our society tries to sneak fruit into cake. We're given mince pies, and we eat them because it helps us "feel Christmassy" but inside we shudder knowing that we've probably accidentally had one of our five a day in that sickly mess of gloopy raisins. A fruit loaf anyone? No thanks. And don't even get me started on Christmas pudding. I need more custard than pudding in my bowl to get through it!

But the saving grace of Christmas snacking is that for about ten days, you can walk into just about any house in the country and locate a box of Celebrations – at least you can in the UK! Of course other chocolate selections sometimes make an appearance too, but Celebrations are everywhere. Normally though our initial excitement at discovering the shiny circular red tub of hope is destroyed when we open the lid. Nearly all the little miniature versions of our favourite chocolate bars are gone. What remains? You guessed it – the little Snickers and the Bounty.

Other people have got there first and enjoyed the wonderful nectar of the Maltesers. The mini Mars Bars and Milky Ways have been scoffed. In a feat of holiday desperation even the miniature Twixes have been gobbled up. But no one wanted the nuts. So they sit there at the bottom of the barrel, pitiful and hopeless. Which is exactly how you feel when you discover once again that they're all that remain.

When it comes to God, it's easy to see him just like a box of Celebrations. We dive in and grab hold of his love; we're delighted to find his kindness, his grace and his patience. We'll go for his instructions at a push. But we act like we can just leave his judgement at the bottom of the tin. We might even be tempted to leave the whole Old Testament there and stick with Jesus and the Gospels.

"I'm more of a New Testament sort of person," we say. "I don't want a God who sends plagues and armies to kill people."

If we're honest, lots of us have a real struggle understanding how the God we meet in Bible books like Judges and Joshua is the same as the God who walked around the streets of Jerusalem chatting with the twelve disciples. We can't square up how God can do things like destroy the enemies of his people, sometimes whole cities of men, women and children, and yet be the same as the God who rescued the woman about to be stoned to death in John 8.

Jesus seems so full of life, kindness, patience, forgiveness and grace! He makes wine at a wedding, heals the sick, feeds the hungry, casts out demons, cures the blind, never fights back, and even dies in the place of others. Elsewhere he demonstrates awesome power and flattens those who oppose him.

How can that be the same God?

If these are your questions, or these are things that your mates say to you or that get thrown at you in RE or Philosophy classes, I totally, totally get it. What we do with these questions really matters. Is God actually good after all? How can we claim that he is who he is when he's done what he's done?

Well, the answer is "simple".

Because God, at his very core, is simple.

You might have just read that and thought: "What?! No he isn't! How can God be simple when he's meant to be just about the biggest thing ever?" That's exactly how I felt the first time I heard about this too.

Honestly.

I thought it sounded like nonsense, and actually quite offensive to call the creator and sustainer of the universe simple. Bit rude tbf.

But don't misunderstand me, I don't mean that God is somehow lacking. He made everything. And he owns everything. And he rules everything. And he always will. Remember, not a blade of grass grows without him telling it to. The most complicated computer humans have ever designed is a drop in the ocean compared to the intelligence of God. The cleverest human ever has about as much of chance of outsmarting God than a sheep does of taking out a skyscraper. (Sheep are really thick. Seriously, YouTube "stupid sheep". It's hilarious.)

God isn't dumb. When we say that God is simple that isn't what we mean at all.

God's simplicity is about who he is. Deep down. At his core. God isn't a complicated mash-up of different attributes or characteristics slotted together. Everything he says and does, flows directly from who he is.

You can get a very different version of me depending on how you catch me. Some days I'm feeling great and I'll be cracking jokes, other days I'm low and more withdrawn. And you just don't want to be around me when I'm tired, stressed or hungry. I'm all over the place. We all change depending on our moods, our priorities or our circumstances, but God doesn't.

God is just 100% God. He's 100% loving and just and holy and everything else he is. All the time. All at once. No separate parts. Simple.

* * *

When I was 11, I went on one of those end of primary school residentials. Mine was back in the year 2000. The fourth Harry Potter book had just come out, they were still making the show *Friends* and reality TV was a new idea. And, most importantly, I was on a school trip. We went to a place called Crystal Palace National Sports Centre. It was an enormous complex and you could do just about every sport you'd heard of, and a few that you hadn't. I remember looking at the map and seeing football pitches, tennis courts, swimming pools, an athletics track, javelin, hockey and a trampoline centre, and thinking "Wow!"

We got to choose what we wanted to try. I remember circling the football, the archery, the cricket and a few other things. But I wasn't interested in the gymnastics stuff or the running tracks. That didn't matter; there were so many options, and no one could choose all of them anyway.

When it comes to God, it's easy to see him a bit like that. We imagine he is this incredibly intricate and complicated being, made-up of loads of different parts. If we mapped him out, we could see his love in the top corner, and his mercy in the middle, and his justice down at the bottom. But we can't be like a fussy child choosing what we want and what we don't want. That's not how God works. You get all of God or nothing. Think blended food not a buffet. God isn't a combination of ten different parts that we can take or leave. He's not a Lego man where you can switch out his head, his body and his legs. He's just God all the time.

So what about the whole Old Testament God versus New Testament God thing?

Well God doesn't fundamentally change when Jesus enters the world. He doesn't change at all. In fact sending Jesus was always the plan (see Ephesians 1:4). The God who gives water to the woman at the well is the same God who allows the Red Sea to close up over the Egyptian Army. And if we've got the idea that Jesus is somehow the gentle version of God the Father then we haven't read the New Testament as carefully as we might think we have.

For example, Acts 17 tells us that it is Jesus who will return to judge all people. The book of Revelation makes it very clear that those who don't trust in Jesus will be held to account for the things they have done and Jesus is pretty frightening to say the least: he has eyes like blazing fire and his voice is as deafening as the crashing torrent of a raging waterfall (see Revelation 1:12–16).

If we're tempted to reject God because of how he judged his enemies in the past, we need to know that he has not finished defeating evil. He's barely getting started. He will wipe all evil from the face of the earth one day. And while that is wonderful, it's also scary.

Scary because the truth is that we all have evil inside of us too. None of us like to admit it but we all have moments where we shock ourselves with how selfish, unkind and heartless we can be. The only way we can be safe from the right justice of a holy God is to ask for his forgiveness and trust that Jesus has made a way for us to be saved by dying in our place on the cross. Maybe you've been reading this book trying to work out what you think about God, whether you're interested in him, whether he's worth following.

The truth is he has done everything that is needed for you to be saved. All you have to do is accept his love, call on his name, and he will save you from his judgement. And he is ready and waiting to hear your prayers today. He's not being slow to come back to the world, he's waiting patiently to give us time to turn to him.

And when you do, because he's simple, you can be sure he is completely dependable and consistent. He'll never have an off day or change his mind about you.

So what?

When we talk about God, we divide up his attributes all the time; we've done that here in this book! We've taken his love, his sovereignty, his jealousy, his self-sufficiency and we've examined those characteristics one by one.

For us as humans to begin to understand who God is, we have to think about him in different ways at different times. That's just one of the limitations of being a human. Just like we can't fit a whole pizza in our mouths all at once so we slice it up into ten tremendous tasty triangles, our brains can't process all of who God is at once. But it's good to step back and remind ourselves we don't have ten pizza slices. We have one incredible God.

It's also good to remind ourselves that, as humans who eat our pizza slice by slice, we experience God in different ways at different times. And that can be really confusing. There are times when we feel like God is there, we have confidence about him, we feel like we want to talk to him, and we can even get this sense of him being with us (which is hard to explain but beautiful to experience). We can see that he is good and kind, and that he has a plan for us. It all seems to click, and it's just marvellous.

But there are times when he feels a million miles away. When our doubts are bigger than our beliefs; when our fears our louder than our faith. When our circumstances change and we feel absolutely heartbroken and totally disorientated. The days when the medical diagnosis comes and we are in bits. When it's depression. When our parents divorce.

When we've failed the exam we gave everything to. When the relationship ends and we had put all our hopes on it.

I've been there, it sucks. God doesn't feel all that good or kind or in charge then. He feels mean, spiteful, callous and we start to wonder if he even exists after all. We've all felt that right?

But God is simple. And this is just about the most comforting truth imaginable.

He's the same God on the day our dreams come true as he is on the day the sky falls in. He isn't one thing one day and a different thing the next. He isn't full of contradictions and inconsistencies like we often are. He's always the same.

That means his love for you is as big on the worst day as it is on the best day. And he's every bit as bothered about ending suffering and evil on the days when it hurts the most as when we're enjoying a leisurely ice cream on the beach. He's still ruling and reigning even when it feels like he isn't. He can't not reign. He is all that he is, turned up to the max, all the time.

That doesn't mean we'll always understand what he's doing, but we can know he never dials down his love or his justice or his holiness. He does what he does because he is who he is. He always has. He always will. If something is true of God today, it's true of God tomorrow. And ten thousand years ago. And in a millennia. He's not hiding some dark secret in his character. We will never discover he's not so loving or perfect or good after all. He is there, he is fair, and he does care.

God is simple so we can trust him.

Conclusion

Why Should I Bother With God?

If you've ever been cancelled you'll know it's a really horrible experience. You go from being close with someone – good mates, always up for message exchange, hanging out all the time – to no response whatsoever. Like you don't exist. Just ghosted. It's really painful, especially when you feel like if only you could talk about it, then the issue would be sorted. But they won't give you the time of day.

Cancel culture is massive. People get cancelled all the time. They no longer fit; they no longer belong.

Rejected. Not welcome. Not listened to anymore. It's almost as if the person has died – they just cease to matter. It's brutal.

We see it all the time with celebrities – someone says or does something (or is perceived to have done something) that is problematic or wrong, and that's it.

Sometimes there are good reasons: someone does something appalling or we discover a terrible secret, and all the prestige and influence their fame had previously given them is taken away.

But sometimes cancelling happens over a misunderstanding or when someone holds views that aren't popular. Society as a collective, or at least the sharp-tongued social media trolls, close them down. They're over. Hounded off on social media; no longer welcome on TV. Gone.

We see it all the time in corridors, classrooms and group chats too. Someone messes up and they're out. We don't understand someone, so we ignore them. Someone comes along who is confusing or just different to us, and we decide it's just easier to have nothing to do with them.

So many people do this to God.

We reject him without taking the time to get to know much about him. We cast him aside without taking the time to properly understand who he is because we've decided he's too different or difficult.

We allow surface-level arguments against him to totally rule him out. We see that he does things like judge evil or allow suffering, and decide that we want nothing more to do with him.

Perhaps you can identify. It's possible that you've been teetering on the edge of doing that very thing. It's possible that you've been in danger of rejecting a God that you don't know that much. That's a huge part of why this book exists: to introduce you to the God you're weighing up or to help you get to know the God that you already follow better. I wrote this book because I'm passionate that we resist the urge to cancel God based on misunderstandings or lack of information.

* * *

Imagine you've got a really close mate, and one day, out of the blue, another friend tells you that he's mates with her too. You're delighted until you ask him a couple of questions and you quickly realise he doesn't know her at all. He just says he does, but he doesn't have any idea about all the things that make her who she is. All he's got is some random garbled second-hand stuff. It's super weird.

We can't claim to know God, if we don't know who he is. And we'll never understand what he does or doesn't do in the world, if we don't seek to understand him – because he does what he does, because he is who he is.

It's easy to massively oversimplify God in our heads and not really do the hard work of finding out what he's really like. But when we do that we end up making God in our own image, rather than seeing the true reality that we have been made in his image.

So well done for doing the hard work of reading this book and going deeper into who God actually is. If you're still struggling to know where you're at with all this God stuff, let me encourage you not to cancel him because he feels too different or to oversimplify him because he seems too difficult. Instead, keep getting to know him. Remember, the reason God spoke this world into being in the first place was to make a place for the people he created so he could love them. God wants to be known!

We see this throughout the Bible. He walked in the garden with Adam and Eve, he led Abraham out under the stars, he wrestled with Jacob, he pursued Moses, he called Gideon, he whispered to Elijah, he restored Ruth, he empowered Esther and then, after that all, he went even further. He put on flesh and entered our world in the person of Jesus. He fed the hungry, cured the diseased, healed the blind, sought out the broken and the marginalised and the forgotten, and wanted to know you (yes, you reading this) so much he even went to the cross, dying to make a way to have a relationship with you.

And he hasn't forgotten you. Jesus might have ascended this earth but God is not absent here, he is present by his Spirit. You can know God today, you can experience his love, light and presence in your life. You can know his peace even when our human understanding dictates you should have no peace. You can know his joy even amid the despair and hopelessness all around us. You can know his freedom even when you feel totally trapped.

God is love. God is Three-in-One. God is Creator. God is different. God is holy. God is sovereign. God is jealous. God is simple. *And this God can be known as a friend by all of us.* He isn't distant; he's present. He's constant. He's a surging waterfall of love and blessing and hope and joy, and because of Jesus we can experience every drop of his goodness and kindness in our lives.

No matter what we are facing we can talk to him, listen to him speak to us in his Word, and hold tightly to his love in the storms of life.

So just before we come into land, let me ask you some questions.

Do you know this God for yourself?

If your answer is no, then let me gently ask – why wouldn't you want to know him? He made you, he loves you, he sent his Son Jesus to die so that you could be saved from your sin, he cares more about you than I can wrap words around. You'd be mad to turn him away. And if you're ready to commit yourself to him today, then your next step is really simple. You can pray something like this:

> "God in heaven, thank you for making me. Thank you for sending Jesus to die so that I can be forgiven of my sin. I want to know you, and to live my life knowing you and following you. Please help me to do that. Amen."

If you've prayed this then welcome to God's family!

Now you're going to need a few things: firstly a Bible if you don't have one already. Every time we read the Bible God speaks, so read one and he'll speak to you! Why not start with the book of Mark (it's near the middle). Mark is the shortest of the four historical accounts about Jesus and it's brilliant. And as you hear him speak, you can talk straight back to him in prayer.

Then you'll need a church. If your family are Christians go to church with them, if not find a church near to you where they love the Bible, love Jesus and love each other. And go. You'll need Christian community to keep living for Jesus.

Do you want to know God better?

Maybe you already trust in God, you've got a Bible and you go to church, but it's hard. None of it feels easy. God feels far off, church is hard work and your Bible is gathering dust. I've had times like that. But the thing is, we can know God, in a real dependable, perfectly normal sort of way. God tells us in James 4:8 that if we draw near to him, he will draw near to us. I've always found that to be true.

So tell him how you feel. The Psalms are full of honest prayers, why not pray one of those. You could say, "God I'm really struggling. It doesn't feel like you're there a lot of the time. Please help! Show me your love, draw near to me by your Spirit, speak to me as I read the Bible. Help me to get to know you better. Thank you that you listen. Amen."

Try that and see what happens. Crack open the Bible again – you could start with Mark too if you're unsure where to go. Keep praying until it gets easier. Commit to your church. Find a Christian friend and do life together.

And keep reading and learning about God. There's always more of God to explore.

We'll never reach the limit of the beautiful, incredible, astonishing things to discover about God because he has no limits. That's just who he is.

Acknowledgments

With special thanks to:

Chris Stead, for his exceptional lectures at Oak Hill College on the Doctrine of God.

The Keswick Week 1 Youth Team who shared and shaped the first iteration of this material in July 2022. Especially Joe, Paul, Ciara and Steve.

My wife Katie, along with the leadership team and church family at St Anne's Church, Grantham. Without your encouragement and support this book would never have happened.